Find It on a
CORAL
REEF

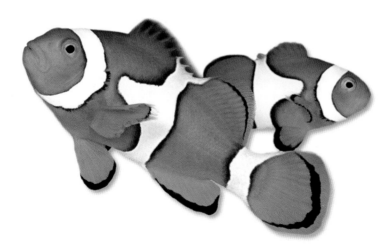

Dee Phillips

GARETH**STEVENS**
GS
PUBLISHING
A Member of the WRC Media Family of Companies

Please visit our web site at: **www.garethstevens.com**
For a free color catalog describing Gareth Stevens Publishing's list of high-quality books
and multimedia programs, call 1-800-542-2595 (USA) or 1-800-387-3178 (Canada).
Gareth Stevens Publishing's fax: (414) 332-3567.

Library of Congress Cataloging-in-Publication Data

Phillips, Dee, 1967-
    Find it on a coral reef / by Dee Phillips.
        p. cm. — (Can you find it?)
    ISBN 0-8368-6302-X (lib. bdg.)
    1. Coral reef ecology—Juvenile literature.   I. Title.
    QL125.P48   2006
    578.77'89—dc22   2005056343

This North American edition first published in 2006 by
Gareth Stevens Publishing
A Member of the WRC Media Family of Companies
330 West Olive Street, Suite 100
Milwaukee, WI 53212 USA

This U.S. edition copyright © 2006 by Gareth Stevens, Inc. Original edition copyright © 2005 by
ticktock Entertainment Ltd. First published in Great Britain in 2005 by ticktock Media Ltd., Unit 2,
Orchard Business Centre, North Farm Road, Tunbridge Wells, Kent TN2 3XF.

Gareth Stevens series editor: Dorothy L. Gibbs
Gareth Stevens graphic designer: Charlie Dahl
Gareth Stevens art direction: Tammy West

Picture credits: (t=top, b=bottom, l=left, r=right, c=center)
Alamy: 6l. CORBIS: 3, 13. FLPA: 1, 2, 4-5, 6-7c, 9, 10, 16, 18-19c, 20-21b.
Every effort has been made to trace the copyright holders for the pictures used in this book.
We apologize in advance for any unintentional omissions and would be pleased to insert the
appropriate acknowledgements in any subsequent edition.

Printed in the United States of America

1 2 3 4 5 6 7 8 9 10 09 08 07 06

Words that appear in the glossary are printed in
boldface type the first time they occur in the text.

Contents

A Coral Reef

There is so much to see on a coral reef, from fascinating fish darting between the corals to sea animals **lumbering** along the bottom.

What can you find on a coral reef?

Lobster

Shark

Sea snake

Sponge

Jellyfish

Sea Turtle

Clown fish

Lion fish

Sea anemone

Lobsters are unusual-looking creatures that live at the bottom of the ocean. A lobster has a soft body that is **protected** by a hard shell.

The eyes of a lobster are at the ends of long **stalks.**

A lobster moves by using both its legs and its tail.

A lobster has five pairs of legs. Its two front legs are much bigger and heavier than the others.

Pincers on the ends of a lobster's front legs act like a finger and a thumb. They help the lobster hold on to its **prey**.

A lobster's front legs are called claws.

Shark

A shark is a type of fish that has a long body and very sharp teeth. The most dangerous kind of shark is the great white shark.

Sharks use their teeth to attack prey. Shark teeth are sharp enough to tear flesh easily.

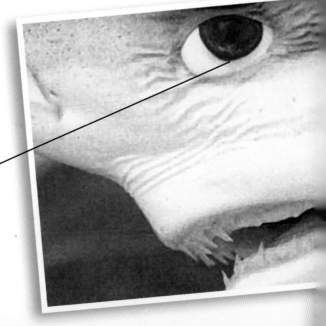

Hunting at night is easy for a shark. Its eyes are much more **sensitive** to light than human eyes.

A shark's bullet-shaped body helps it cut through water swiftly and smoothly. The shark uses its fins to steer and to stay balanced in the water.

Sea Snake

Sea snakes live in shallow water and come up to the surface to breathe air. Their nostrils close up when they are under the water.

There are more than fifty different kinds of sea snakes, and all of them are poisonous.

Sea snakes are good swimmers. The ends of their tails are flat, like paddles, to help them swim.

A sea snake has short **fangs** in its mouth that **inject** poison into its prey. Sea snakes can open their mouths wide enough to bite a person's leg.

Sponge

A sponge looks a lot like a plant, but it is actually a simple form of animal. Sponges can be found on the seabed.

Some sea sponges are collected and sold to people to use the same way they would use a manufactured sponge.

The surface of a sponge is covered with holes called ostia. The ostia suck in the tiny ocean creatures the sponge eats.

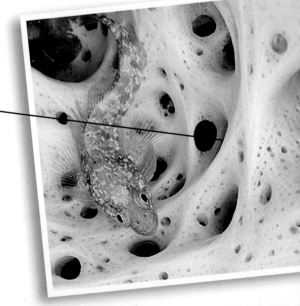

Sponges attach themselves to something hard on the seafloor and then never move again.

Jellyfish

There are many different kinds of jellyfish. The smallest jellyfish is only a few inches (centimeters) across. The largest can be more than a 1 yard (1 meter) wide.

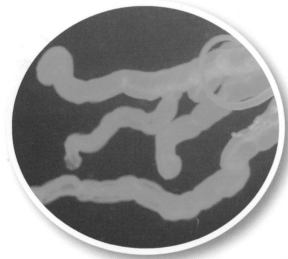

Jellyfish have long, flowing **tentacles**. When the tentacles touch another animal, they sting!

The mouth of a jellyfish is under its body. Along with its armlike tentacles, a jellyfish also has **oral** arms, which it uses to put food into its mouth.

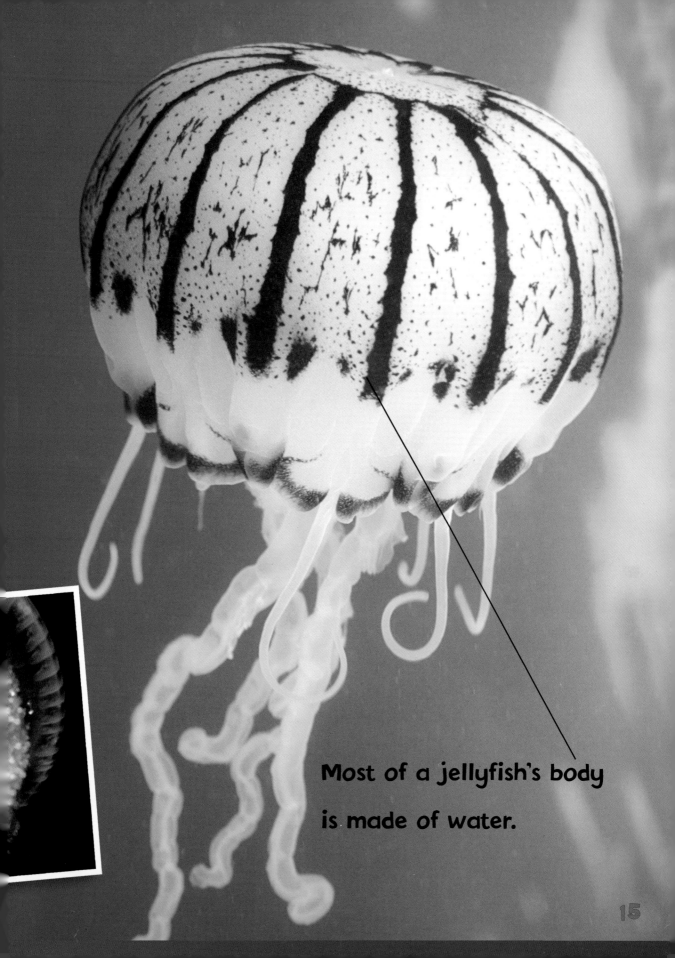

Most of a jellyfish's body
is made of water.

Sea Turtle

Turtles are found in oceans all over the world. The largest kinds of sea turtles weigh more than 1,100 pounds (500 kilograms).

A sea turtle has a thick, hard shell that protects its soft body.

Sea turtles have **flippers** instead of legs so they can swim very well. On land, however, they move very slowly.

Male sea turtles almost never come out of the water. Females usually come on land only to lay eggs.

Sea turtles lay their eggs in the sand. They use their front flippers to dig holes and to bury the eggs. A female turtle can lay up to one hundred eggs.

Clown Fish

This tiny, colorful fish has a special friendship with sea anemones. Clown fish live in warm oceans, wherever sea anemones are found.

The name "clown fish" comes from the bright markings on its body, which look a lot like clown makeup.

The fish's markings **attract** creatures for the sea anemone to eat.

A coating of **mucus** on its body, protects the clown fish from the sea anemone's sting.

Clown fish usually live in pairs. The female fish lays her eggs on rocks that are very near the sea anemone.

Lion Fish

Striped lion fish have poisonous spines all around their bodies. These fish live in holes and caves in coral reefs and come out at night to hunt for food.

Lion fish usually live alone or in small family groups.

The poisonous spines on a lion fish help protect the fish from **predators**.

Most of the time, lion fish swim slowly, but they can swim fast when they attack.

Sea Anemone

A sea anemone is an animal that looks like a flower. It spends its life attached to the ocean floor and can grow to a height of about 6 feet (2 m).

There are many different kinds of sea anemones. Some of them are very colorful.

The body of a sea anemone is shaped like a **column**. Its mouth is at the top of the column.

Clown fish help sea anemones by attracting ocean creatures for the anemones to eat. The clown fish eat the anemones' leftovers.

Glossary

attract – invite others to come near by looking appealing or interesting

column – a tall, round structure that looks like a pole

fangs – hollow, pointed teeth used for biting and injecting poison

flippers – the paddlelike body parts on some animals that swim

inject – to squirt a liquid into an object through a pointed instrument, such as a needle

lumbering – moving very slowly and often awkwardly

mucus – a slimy coating that protects the skin of some animals and helps keep them from drying out

oral – having to do with the mouth

pincers – claws made up of two sections that open and close

predators – animals that hunt and kill other animals for food

prey – an animal that is killed by another animal for food

protected – kept safe from harm

sensitive – able to sense things very easily

stalks – long, thin stems

tentacles – long, armlike growths on the bodies of some sea animals